MAH LA'ASOT

WHAT SHOULD I DO?

A BOOK OF ETHICAL AND JEWISH RESPONSES

JANICE ALPER & JOEL LURIE GIRSHAVER

ILLUSTRATED BY JACKIE URBANOVIC

TORAH AURA PRODUCTIONS

ISBN 10 #1-934527-38-6
ISBN 13 #978-1-934527-38-2

Copyright © 1992 Janice Alper
Second Edition

Published by Torah Aura Productions
Torah Aura Productions
4423 Fruitland Avenue
Los Angeles, California 90058
(800) BE-TORAH (213) 585-7312

MANUFACTURED IN CHINA

contents

Unit I: *Pikuah Nefesh*—The Drownings 5
  Problem 1: The Drowning Person. 5
  Problem 2: The Old Refrigerator. 9
  Problem 3: The Drowning Dog 11
    A Story 14
  Problem 4: A Drowning Person and a Drowning Animal 15
  Problem 5: Shoot the Dog 17
    Test Cases 19
  The Drownings—A Summary 20

Unit II: *Sakanah*—Some Dangerous Situations. 5
  Problem 6: Angel Doom Risk 21
  Problem 7: The Non-Swimmer 23
  Problem 8: The Suez Canal Bather 25
  Problem 9: Dr. Death. 27
    Test Cases 31
  Dangerous Situations—Summary 32

Unit III: *Shmirat Shabbat*—Observing the Sabbath 33
  Problem 10: The Natural Disaster 37
    A Story 39
    Health Care 40
  Problem 11: The Muddy Horse 41
  Problem 12: The Accident 43
  Problem 13: The Power Line 45

Unit IV: *Nefesh Mip'nei Nefesh*—Issues of Self Defense 5
  Problem 14: The Armed Burglar 47
  Problem 15: Are You a Hero 49
  Problem 16: Go Ahead, Make My Day .51
  Problem 17: One Canteen of Water 53
  Problem 18: Kill Or Be Killed 55
    Test Cases. 57
    Two Talmudic Stories. 58
  Problem 19: A Pregnant Mother 59
  Problem 20: Abortion Complications 61
  Issues of Self Defense—Summary 64

UNIT I:
פִּקוּחַ־נֶפֶשׁ

Pikuah Nefesh—The Drowinings
PROBLEM 1: THE DROWNING PERSON

You and a group of your friends have ridden bicycles to a lake that is near a friend's house. After a while, you realize it is getting late and is time to go home. As you prepare to leave, you notice that one of your group is missing. You turn around to see him struggling in the water. He may be drowning.

Mah la'asot? **What should you do?** _____

_____

What is your responsibility in this matter? _____

_____

Why do you have a responsibility in this matter? _____

_____

THE DROWNING PERSON—
THE JEWISH ANSWER

Problem: If you see a person who may be hurt or killed, what should you do?

Answer: If you are not putting your own life at risk, you must try to save the other person.

Reason: The obligation to save another person is based on a principle in *Halakhah* (Jewish Law) called *Pikuah Nefesh,* saving a soul. Protecting a human life is a major Jewish obligation.

Our rabbis learned this lesson from two different places in the Torah:

> DO NOT STAND IDLY BY THE BLOOD OF YOUR NEIGHBOR. (Leviticus 19:16)

The first verse (Leviticus 19:16) teaches us that as Jews we are not allowed to stand by and watch someone else be injured or killed. That would be "STANDING IDLY BY THE BLOOD OF YOUR NEIGHBOR." If someone is going to be hurt or killed, a Jew is responsible to try to prevent this injury or death.

> YOU SHALL KEEP MY LAWS AND RULES,
> YOU SHALL ACT ON THEM,
> PEOPLE SHALL LIVE BY THEM. (Leviticus 18:5)

The second verse (Leviticus 18:5) teaches us a second lesson. The key words are "PEOPLE SHALL **LIVE** BY THEM." Even though Jews are supposed to do all the *mitzvot* (because they are commandments), one should not perform a *mitzvah* if it would mean dying. This means that if it is likely that you will die trying, you should not attempt to save another person. If you don't know how to swim very well, you should not swim out after a drowning person.[1]

Why should a Jew try to save another person's life? _____

_____

When should a Jew not try to save a person who is drowning? Why? _____

_____

---

[1]A person who is drowning often panics. Sometimes, he/she can drown the person who is trying to save him/her. If you haven't studied lifesaving and you don't know how to approach a drowning swimmer, you shouldn't go in after one. It is much safer to throw the person a float, push a board out to him/her, etc. Not knowing how to help can easily put your own life at risk.

Jewish legal texts teach:

> The phrase, "DO NOT STAND IDLY BY THE BLOOD OF YOUR NEIGHBOR" means "Do not watch without doing something while your neighbor's blood is shed." If you see someone in danger of drowning in the river, being carried away by wild beasts, or being attacked by robbers, you must try to rescue that person. (Sifra on Lev. 19:16)

Which of these people correctly practiced Pikua<u>h</u> Nefesh, saving a soul? Circle their numbers.

1. Randy gave five dollars to the Cancer Society. Randy is nine years old.

2. Sam never learned CPR (cardiopulmonary resuscitation). One day, when his little cousin fell into the pool and started to drown, Sam pulled her out. When Sam saw that she wasn't breathing, he did his best. He blew in her mouth and pushed on her stomach the way he had seen characters on television do it. Sam is fourteen years old.

3. Twelve-year-old Erica is driving with her mother. She sees a tattered street person lying on the ground. He appears to be unconscious. She tells her mother to stop. Her mother says, "No, he's just an old drunk."

4. Every year the synagogue has a blood drive to collect blood for the Red Cross. Every year, Debby's mother makes a point of being one of the first to sign up.

5. Aviva is a good swimmer. She is picnicking by the lake when she sees that Tom (who is also swimming) has a cramp and may be in trouble. Rather than jumping in to help him, she grabs the Styrofoam ice chest from the people on the next blanket, dumps out their food, runs out on the dock, and tosses the ice chest near Tom. It floats, he grabs it, and he catches his breath. Aviva is seventeen years old.

6. There is an automobile accident in front of Bob's house. Bob is out front playing on the steps. He sees that someone is hurt. He runs inside, calls 911 and reports the accident. Then he runs to the car to see if he can help. Bob is ten years old.

PROBLEM 2: THE OLD REFRIGERATOR

We know that we are responsible to save a person who is in danger, but do we have a responsibility to prevent possible danger?

You are walking home from school one day. In the front yard of one of the houses down the street, you see an old refrigerator. The owner has not bothered to take the door off. Rather, he has just loosely tied a rope around it. You see that a bunch of little kids are playing hide-and-go-seek down the street.[2]

Mah la'asot? What should you do? _____

_____

Do you have a responsibility in this matter? _____

_____

---

[2]Many children have died from playing in refrigerators. When the door is closed, a refrigerator is completely airtight. There is no way of opening the door from the inside. It most states it is illegal to put a refrigerator out without removing the door.

THE OLD REFRIGERATOR—
THE JEWISH ANSWER

Problem: An unused refrigerator, which can be dangerous to young children, is left outside by somebody else. When no one is actually at risk, do you have to do something in order to prevent possible harm?

Answer: Yes! This too is a question of *Pikuah Nefesh*. By protecting children from the possible danger of being accidentally trapped in a refrigerator, you are avoiding "STANDING IDLY BY THE BLOOD OF YOUR NEIGHBOR," and you may be saving a soul.

Reason: The rabbis learned the concept of "prevention" as mitzvah from a rule in the Torah about making roofs.

> WHEN YOU BUILD A NEW HOUSE,
> YOU MUST PUT A PARAPET AROUND THE ROOF. (Deuteronomy 22:8)

A "parapet" is a wall around a roof. In ancient Israel, all roofs were flat, and people used them the way we use porches and balconies. The parapets kept people from falling off. They prevented accidents. From this specific law in the Torah, the rabbis learned that it is a *mitzvah* to try to prevent all accidents where people could be hurt or killed.

The *Kitzur Shulhan Arukh* is a handbook of Jewish laws. It says:

> Not only roofs must be made safe against danger to human life, but any place where there could be an accident....One must put a wall around an open well or a pit, and one must not leave a broken ladder standing where a person could use it, and the same can be said about keeping a vicious dog. *(Kitzur Shulhan Arukh, Book 4, 190:1–2)*

List five other things which a responsible person should do to apply the lesson taught by the parapet.

1. _____

2. _____

3. _____

4. _____

5. _____

PROBLEM 3: THE DROWNING DOG

It is a mitzvah to save a human life, but do we have a responsibility to save an animal which is at risk?

As you leave the lake, it is not your friend you see in the lake, but his dog. The dog is obviously struggling for air and appears to be drowning.

Mah la'asot? What should you do? _____

_____

Is it your responsibility to save the dog? Defend your answer. _____

_____

THE DROWNING DOG—THE JEWISH ANSWER

Problem: Your friend's dog is drowning. Do you have an obligation to save an animal?

Answer: Here, too, the Jewish answer is exactly the same as with a person. If your own life will not be put at risk, you must save the dog.

Reason: There is a Jewish value called *Tza'ar Ba'alei Hayyim,* preventing the pain of living creatures. The rabbis learned it from several passages they found in the Torah.

> IF YOU SEE YOUR ENEMY'S DONKEY
> STRUGGLING UNDER A LOAD WHICH IS TOO HEAVY
> YOU MUST LIFT THE BURDEN FROM THE DONKEY. (Exodus 23:5)

> IF YOU SEE YOUR FRIEND'S DONKEY OR OX
> FALLEN ON THE ROAD,
> DO NOT IGNORE IT;
> YOU MUST HELP HIM RAISE IT. (Deuteronomy 22:4)

One of these laws talks about the animal of an enemy. The other talks about the animal of a friend. When we put the two laws together we learn an important lesson: it is the animal which must be helped, regardless of who owns it. This is the mitzvah of *Tza'ar Ba'alei Hayyim,* preventing the pain of animals.

Why do you think our rabbis were concerned for the welfare of animals? _____

_____

What is similar about rescuing a person and an animal? _____

_____

What responsibilities do you have when you see an animal in pain or danger? _____

_____

There is an organization called the S.P.C.A. (Society for the Prevention of Cruelty to Animals). What is the purpose of this organization? With what Jewish value is this organization concerned?

Here are three other laws in the Torah which have to do with *Tza'ar Ba'alei Ḥayyim,* preventing cruelty to animals. Read them.

DO NOT MUZZLE AN OX WHEN YOU MAKE IT WORK IN A FIELD OF GRAIN. (Deuteronomy 25:4)

Why would muzzling an ox when it works in a field be cruel? _____

_____

What other rules could you write to cover other times when a person might inflict pain on an animal in a similar way? _____

_____

YOU SHALL NOT PLOW WITH AN OX AND A DONKEY YOKED TOGETHER. (Deuteronomy 22:10)

Why would plowing with an ox and a donkey together be cruel? _____

_____

What other rules could you write to cover other times when a person might inflict pain on an animal in a similar way? _____

_____

WHEN YOU ARE WALKING ON THE ROAD AND YOU FIND A BIRD'S NEST...WITH EGGS OR YOUNG CHICKS AND THE MOTHER IS GUARDING THEM...DO NOT TAKE THE MOTHER AND HER YOUNG TOGETHER. LET THE MOTHER GO AND ONLY TAKE THE YOUNG. (Deuteronomy 22:6–7)

Why would taking both the mother and her young be cruel? _____

_____

Why can't you leave the young and take the mother? _____

_____

What other rules could you write to cover other times when a person might inflict pain on an animal in a similar way? _____

_____

13

A STORY

In the Midrash, this story is told about Rabbi Judah the Prince, the editor of the Mishnah.

Once Rabbi Judah the prince sat and taught Torah before the academy in Sepphoris, Babylonia. While he was teaching, a calf who was supposed to be slaughtered came in and hid under his robes. It began to moo, seeming to say, "Please save me." Rabbi Judah said to the calf, "What can I do for you? You were created to be eaten."

For the next thirteen years, Rabbi Judah suffered from the same toothache constantly.

One day a lizard ran past his daughter. She wanted to kill it. Rabbi Judah said to her, "Let it be, because it says in the Bible, 'God has mercy over all of God's creations."

At that moment it was said in heaven, "Because he had pity, pity shall be shown to him." The toothache finally stopped. (Genesis Rabbah, Noah 33:3)

What is the moral of this story? _____

_____

Why do you think the Rabbis told a story about a time when one of their heroes was cruel to an animal? _____

_____

_____

PROBLEM 4: A DROWNING PERSON and a DROWNING ANIMAL

It is a mitzvah to save the life of a person. It is also a mitzvah to prevent an animal from suffering. What happens if a person has to choose between these two mitzvot?

You go to the lake for a third time. This time you see both a person and a dog drowning. You will only have time to save one.

Mah la'asot? **What should you do?** _____

_____

On what did you base your decision? _____

_____

How do you feel about the decision you made? _____

_____

A DROWNING PERSON AND A DROWNING ANIMAL—THE JEWISH ANSWER

Problem: You see both a person and a dog drowning. You only have time to save one of them. What should you do?

Answer: You must save the person (providing your own life will not be at risk).

Reason: While people have an obligation to prevent animals from suffering, they have a greater obligation to save human life.

Our tradition teaches us that *Pikua_h_ Nefesh* is more important than Tza'ar *Ba'alei Hayyim.*

Tza'ar Ba'alei Hayyim means that we must prevent an animal from suffering. *Pikua_h_ Nefesh* means saving a soul. The Jewish tradition believes that people have souls and that animals do not. Animals are important and should be treated well; people *must* be saved.

Do you agree with the tradition? Defend your answer. _____

_____

Would the situation be different if the person were someone you did not like or did not know and the dog was your friend's pet? Explain your answer. _____

_____

What if the person who was drowning was someone who was known for selling drugs or stealing, and the dog was your pet collie who once saved your life? Would the situation be different? Why?

_____

_____

PROBLEM 5: SHOOT THE DOG

Even though a person's life has first priority, and if we have to choose, we choose to save the person's life over the animal's, can we cause an animal suffering in order to prevent injury to a human?

FIRE WHEN READY, GRISLY.

A medic is a soldier who is not a doctor but who is trained to serve as medical help for soldiers on the battlefield. Well-trained medics can save lots of lives.

For many years it was the practice of the U.S. Army to shoot dogs and then have the medics practice on them. The medics learned how to remove bullets and close wounds by working on injured dogs. The army argued that practicing on real bullet wounds was the only way medics could learn effectively. Animal rights activists argued that this practice was cruel to animals. Eventually this practice was stopped.

If the United States Army had to follow Jewish law, would shooting animals with bullets to let medics practice be a good expression of the mitzvah of *Pikuah Nefesh or* a violation of *Tza'ar Ba'alei Hayyim*? Explain your reasoning.

SHOOT THE DOG—THE JEWISH ANSWER

Problem: What if inflicting pain on an animal saves a human life? Which *mitzvah* should you follow? Can you break *Tza'ar Ba'alei Hayyim* in order to perform *Pikuah Nefesh?*

Answer: Yes, in principle; however, not in this specific case. When we have to choose between an animal's life or an animal's pain and a human life, the Jewish tradition tells us to always choose to save the human. In this case (as you will see below), there is a choice.

Reason: In the *Kitzur Shulhan Arukh* we find this law:

> It is a Torah law that we are forbidden to inflict any pain on an animal. In fact, it is our responsibility to relieve the pain of any animal (no matter who owns it).

> However, if the animal causes trouble, or if the animal is needed for a medical purpose, or for any other human purpose, it is permissible to kill it and ignore the pain.

Based on this much of the law, the answer would seem obvious. The possibility of saving even one human life seems to be a good enough reason to cause the dogs pain. However, the last part of this law teaches us one more insight.

> It is also permissible to kill or hurt animals in order to fulfill the mitzvah of writing a *Sefer Torah* (a Torah Scroll). Therefore, it would be permissible to pluck feathers from a living goose in order to make the quills needed for writing the Torah—if no other pen were available. However, people do not do this (they get their quills in other ways) because this is cruel.

> (Kitzur Shulhan Arukh, Volume 4, Chapter 1:1–1)

This law suggests that even though other *mitzvot* may be more important, if there is a way to avoid causing an animal pain and suffering, it must be avoided.

The Solution: After animal rights activists did a lot of complaining, the army worked out a new solution. Medics were trained on models and then taken to inner city hospitals where (unfortunately) they were able to practice on lots of real bullet wounds inflicted on actual people.

Test Cases

Which of these cases describe circumstances in which one should violate the mitzvah of _Tza'ar Ba'alei Hayyim_ in order to perform the mitzvah of _Pikuah Nefesh_?

1. Killing cows (in a painless manner) in order to eat hamburgers.

2. Inflicting severe pain on laboratory rabbits in order to make sure that a new makeup will not cause harm to the human being who will use it.

3. Taking the heart out of a living and healthy orangutan in order to extend the life of an infant girl with a defective heart, and in order to possibly learn how to save other lives. (This was really done at Loma Linda Hospital in California with a baby girl who was known as "Baby Faye.)

4. Shooting a horse with a broken leg in order to put it out of its misery.

5. Neutering cats in order to prevent them from creating more wild cats.

6. Causing cancer in laboratory chimpanzees to study how cancer takes over a body in order to begin to prepare cures and preventions.

THE DROWNINGS—A SUMMARY

In the last few lessons, you have been looking at situations which deal with saving a life. There were two basic values discussed:

פְּקוּחַ-נֶפֶשׁ *Pikuah Nefesh*, saving a soul.

צַעַר בַּעֲלֵי-חַיִּים *Tza'ar Ba'alei Hayyim*, the pain of living creatures.

You have learned that no matter what, it is most important to go out of your way to save a human life, providing there is no risk to your life.

Take a few minutes and try to think of a situation where would you have to make a decision about *Pikuah Nefesh*. **Write about it in the space below.**

_____

_____

_____

What would you do to solve the problem you have described?

_____

_____

_____

Pikuah Nefesh is a very important Jewish value. The Jewish tradition teaches us that if we save but one human life, it is as if we have saved the whole world. That is the true value of *Pikuah Nefesh,* that saving a soul, even one soul, is as if you have saved the entire world.

UNIT II:
סַכָּנָה
Sakanah—Some Dangerous Situations
PROBLEM 6: ANGEL DOOM RISK

We know that it is a mitzvah to prevent a person from coming to harm, but what should we do if that person intentionally rejects our help?

Angel insists that he doesn't need to wear a helmet when he rides his motorcycle. There is no law in his state that requires it. He is a safe driver and has never had an accident. He hates the confinement, the weight, and the heat of the helmet. It deprives him of the sense of being out in the open and free, and that's what he likes about riding the bike. He isn't putting anyone else in danger, and it is his own choice.

Ally likes Angel. She is his girlfriend. She is worried and wants to protect him from foolish and dangerous actions. She is frightened that one day he will get in an accident (it will probably be someone else's fault) and be badly hurt. She wants him to wear a helmet. He refuses.

Who is right? Defend your answer. _____

_____

Do you think that the Torah has something to say about this? If so, what would Jewish law teach? ___

_____

_____

21

ANGEL DOOM'S RISK—THE JEWISH ANSWER

Problem: Angel's refusal to wear a motorcycle helmet risks his own life and health. It is, however, his own life. Should anyone else be able to make him change his own behavior when it doesn't hurt anyone else?

Answer: According to the ways the Rabbis read the Torah, Angel is not allowed to foolishly put his own life and health at risk. He should be made to protect himself.

Reason: Jews believe that life is a gift from God and that it is wrong for someone to waste that gift. In the Kitzur Shulhan Arukh we learn

> God wants every person to keep his or her body healthy and safe, because only a healthy person can grow in his or her knowledge of the Creator... We learn this from Deuteronomy 4:15, "THEREFORE, TAKE GOOD CARE OF YOURSELF..." (Kitzur Shulhan Arukh, Volume 1, 32:1)

Risking your life is a violation of the mitzvah to "TAKE GOOD CARE OF YOURSELF." Maimonides expands this rule:

> The Rabbis of the Talmud forbid many things because they are dangerous to life. Anyone who ignores these rules and says, "It is only my own life I am risking—no one else can tell me what to do!" should be lashed for disobedience. (Mishneh Torah, Laws of Murder and Life Preservation, Chapter 11:5)

Is Angel correct when he claims that he is only risking his own life, and that no one else will be hurt? Explain.

_____

_____

_____

PROBLEM 7: THE NON-SWIMMER

It is a mitzvah to save a person's life, but what should we do if trying to save another person puts us in grave danger?

One day you are in the mountains, walking near a river. Suddenly you look around and you see a person drowning. You cannot swim.

Mah la'asot? **What should you do?** _____

_____

What is your responsibility in this matter? _____

_____

Why do you have a responsibility in this matter? _____

_____

THE NON-SWIMMER—THE JEWISH ANSWER

Problem: It is a mitzvah, *Pikuah Nefesh*, to save a person who is in danger. It is also a mitzvah not to put your own life in danger. Must you obey the first commandment if it is likely that you will die in the attempt?

Answer: You should do everything possible to save the person, except put your own life at risk.

Reason: Again, we are expected to observe the principle of *Pikuah Nefesh*, saving a soul. However, since you cannot swim, there are other considerations. Now there are two lives in danger, the drowning person's and yours. However, sometimes you have to risk your life in order to save another life.

> In the *Kesef Mishneh*, a commentary on Moses Maimonides' *Mishneh Torah*, a code of Jewish Law, a distinction is made between two levels of danger: *Safek Sakanah*, Possible Danger; and *Vadai Sakanah*, Certain Danger.
>
> סָפֵק סַכָּנָה *Safek Sakanah* is possible danger. If you try to save someone else, it is possible you may get hurt. Under those conditions, a person may (or perhaps should) try to save the other person.
>
> וַדַּאי סַכָּנָה *Vadai Sakanah* is certain danger, where one is likely to be killed. We are forbidden to attempt to save the other person's life if there is a good chance we will be killed. One cannot kill oneself to save another.

In this instance, you are in certain danger, *Vadai Sakanah*, because you do not know how to swim. If you try to save your friend by jumping in the water after him, you will surely drown, and then two lives will be lost.

What are some ways you can change the situation from one of *Vadai Sakanah*, certain danger, to *Safek Sakanah*, possible danger?

_____

_____

_____

PROBLEM 8: THE SUEZ CANAL BATHER

It is a mitzvah to try to save another person (even against that person's will), but do we have to take great risks to save people who foolishly risk their own lives (against our advice)?

In the Yom Kippur War, the Israeli Defense Forces pushed all the way to the Suez Canal. It was very hot. The IDF issued an order prohibiting soldiers from swimming in the canal because they would be easy targets for snipers. Even so, many soldiers violated the order (because it was so hot) and wound up in certain danger. Other soldiers were ordered down to the edge of the canal to provide covering fire to try to save these soldiers who had stupidly put themselves in *Vadai Sakanah*.

This could only happen in Israel. Some of the soldiers thought it was against Jewish law for them to risk their own lives and put themselves in *Safek Sakanah* to rescue people who were stupid and had intentionally put themselves in *Vadai Sakanah*. They obeyed their orders but asked the army rabbis to rule whether in the future such orders were the wrong thing for a the army to ask of a good Jew. The army went and asked a group of rabbinical scholars to answer this *halakhic question*.

If you were the Chief Rabbi of the army, what would you decide? Defend your answer.

_____

_____

THE SUEZ CANAL BATHER—THE JEWISH ANSWER

Problem: Should a person put him or herself in *Safek Sakanah* in order to rescue another person who has intentionally put him or herself in *Vadai Sakanah?*

Answer: Yes, because where the risk is only possible, one is still obligated to perform the *mitzvah* of *Pikuah Nefesh.*

Reason: Rabbi Yehuda Gershuni, a leading Talmudic scholar, wrote the legal decision for the IDF. He said:

> Just because a person foolishly endangers his (or her) own life does not mean that he (or she) has lost God's love, His (or her) body is a gift from God. It belongs to God. Therefore, it is the duty of bystanders not to stand by and just say "it serves him (or her) right" if he or she were killed. (*Or ha-Mizrakh*, World Zionist Organization 21, no. 1)

In another legal opinion, Rabbi Jonathan Emden wrote:

> Just because one's body belongs to God (and acting foolishly might put it at risk) does not relieve a bystander from entering into *Safek Sakanah* in order to save another person. (She'elat, Yavetz, Responsum 43)

MOVIE ENDING

1. In the film *Terminator 2,* T2000, the robot played by Arnold Schwarzenegger, lowers itself into a vat of hot metal in order to destroy all its parts so that its technology will not lead to a nuclear holocaust. Did the T2000 do the right thing? Would Jewish law support its action?

2. In the play *Romeo and Juliet,* Juliet takes a sleeping potion. Romeo thinks she is dead. He doesn't want to live without her. He kills himself. Then, when she wakes up and sees him dead, she feels the same way. She kills herself, too. Is this romantic? Did Romeo and Juliet have the right to decide what to do with their own lives? What would Jewish law say about this action?

3. In the movie *Rambo III,* the character played by Sylvestor Stallone goes into Afghanistan to rescue his old friend, the Colonel, played by Richard Crenna. He is almost certain to die because the mission is all but impossible (even for Rambo). Did Rambo do the right thing? What would Jewish law say about this action?

4. In the movie *Thelma and Louise,* the two women are trapped by the police at the end of the film. Rather than giving in and going to jail, the two women want to remain free, so they drive off a cliff and kill themselves. Did they do the right thing? What would Jewish law say about this action?

5. In the film *Boyz N the Hood,* when the character Doughboy goes out and shoots the gang members who had killed his brother in a drive-by shooting, he faces probable death, either from other gangs or from the police. He gets revenge. Did he do the right thing? What would Jewish law say about this action?

6. In *Dances with Wolves,* the character "Dances with Wolves," played by Kevin Costner, risks his life to save the woman "Stands with a Fist." When he finds she is wounded, he takes her to the tribe (who will probably kill him). Fortunately, they don't. Should he have taken the risk? What would Jewish law say about this action?

PROBLEM 9: DR. DEATH

We know that it is wrong for a person to put his or her own life in danger, and that we have a responsibility to try to save every human life. What happens when a person is in great pain and believes that death would be more of a blessing than continued life?

Dr. Jack Kevorkian is a retired pathologist. In 1990 and 1991, he helped three women commit suicide. In all three cases, the women had contracted diseases which were painful and upsetting but not immediately fatal. Jane Adkins suffered from Alzheimer's disease. She was 54 when she died. Sherry Miller had multiple sclerosis and was 43 when she died. Marjorie Wantz was 58 and suffered from an incurable pelvic disease. In each case, Dr. Kevorkian connected the woman to a device, and she activated it, causing her own death.

Each of these assisted suicides took place in Michigan, where such action was not illegal. In a press release, the doctor's lawyer said, "Dr. Kevorkian believes it is a doctor's responsibility to alleviate pain."

Mah la'asot? **What should be done?** _____

_____

Did Dr. Kevorkian fulfill his obligation to his patients by helping them end their pain? Was this a mitzvah? Explain. _____

_____

What was Dr. Kevorkian's responsibility in this matter?_____

_____

DR. Death—THE JEWISH ANSWER

Problem: If a suffering patient wants to die, may a doctor do something to help him/her end his/her life?

Answer: No! Jewish tradition always considers suicide wrong.

Explanation: Suicide violates the *mitzvah* of *Pikuah Nefesh*. The midrash on Genesis says:

> There is none so wicked as one who commits suicide. This is taught in Genesis 9:5 where it says, "I REQUIRE RESPONSIBILITY FOR EVERY HUMAN LIFE..." For the world was created for only one individual and one who destroys a life (even his or her own) is as one who destroys the whole world. (Genesis Rabbah 34:13)

Personal suffering is not a good enough reason to end one's life and violate the mitzvah of *Pikuah Nefesh*. While the doctor is not guilty of murder, he has done the wrong thing in helping these women waste a portion of the lives which God gave them. In the Shulhan Arukh it says:

> A dying person must be treated as a living person. We may not tie their jaws, nor anoint them with oil, nor wash them, nor remove the pillow from under their heads. We may not prepare the funeral, nor may we close their eyes before the soul departs. One who closes the eyes of a dying person before death is regarded as one who sheds blood. (Yoreh Deah 339:1)

A STORY

When Judah the Prince, the editor of the Mishnah, was dying, the other rabbis decreed public fast days and offered prayers for heavenly mercy. They also announced that anyone who said that Rabbi Judah was as good as dead would be stabbed with a sword.

Rabbi Judah's handmaid went up on the roof and prayed. She said, "The immortals want Rabbi Judah to join them and the mortals want him to remain with them. May it be the will of God that the mortals may overpower the immortals."

Later she saw that he was in much pain. Finally, she changed her prayer and said, "May it be the will of God that the immortals overpower the mortals." The Rabbis, however, continued their prayers for Rabbi Judah's recovery. They never stopped. The woman took up a jar and threw it down from the roof to the ground. For a moment, the Rabbis stopped their prayers. In that pause, Rabbi Judah died and his soul found peace. (Ketubbot 1:4a)

What lesson is taught by this story?

_____

_____

_____

These rules are found in the *Mappah,* a commentary on the *Shulhan Arukh.*

If there is something which prevents the departure of a soul such as the sound of a person chopping wood, or salt on the tongue, we may stop the chopping or remove the salt so as not to hinder the departure of the soul. (Yoreh Deah 339:1)

LiFe anD DeatH DecisiOns

We know that according to Jewish law we may do nothing which causes a person to die, and that in extreme cases we need not do something which unnaturally extends life. According to Jewish medical ethics, what is the right thing to do in each of these cases:

1. A twenty-three-year-old accident victim has been kept alive by a series of machines. The doctors believe she is "brain dead" and that there is no realistic hope of recovery.

2. An eleven-year-old boy has a bad case of the stomach flu. He feels awful. He says that he would rather die than go through any more pain.

3. A sixty-four-year-old woman is diagnosed with a stomach cancer. Without treatment she will be dead within six months. An experimental treatment will keep her alive for two or perhaps three years, but her hair will fall out, she will be in pain much of time, and most of that time will be spent in the hospital.

4. A brain-damaged baby is born to parents who do not want her. Without an operation on her stomach, she will not live once she is taken off the feeding tubes. If the operation is performed and if she lives, she will probably never reach twenty, and most likely will never be able to take care of herself. One doctor wants to perform the operation while another wants to take her off the feeding tubes and let nature take its course. The parents don't care.

5. This is the plot of a movie and Broadway play, *Whose Life Is It Anyway?* A famous sculptor in his forties is in a car crash and becomes a quadriplegic. His mind is perfectly functional—even brilliant—but he cannot move a muscle below his neck. Everything must be done for him. He can easily live in good health and without pain for twenty or more years. But he wants to die, because he feels that he can no longer do anything meaningful. Should he have the right to end his life?

Test cases

Which of these people did the right thing? What does Jewish law say about each of these cases?

1. A spy who swallows a poison pill rather than letting the enemies torture him and get information out of him.

2. A person who lost everything in the stock market and "accidentally" fell out of a 37th-floor window so his family would get some help from his insurance.

3. A Buddhist monk who poured gasoline on himself and burned himself alive to show the world how great was the suffering of his people under a foreign oppressor. (There is a famous photograph of this act taking place.)

4. Samson, who took his own life in order to kill hundreds of Israel's enemies before he died.

5. A person dying of cancer who doesn't want to experience any more pain and who wants her family to have good memories of her rather than those which would come at the end.

6. A doctor who tests an experimental and dangerous drug (which may save many lives) on herself before allowing other patients to try it.

7. A driver who sends her car off the road into the ravine in order to avoid the school bus which has spun out of control on the narrow bridge.

Dangerous Situations—Summary

In this unit, we learned that Jews are not allowed to risk injury or death (because our bodies belong to God Who made them and Who gave us life).

Despite this rule to take care with our bodies and our lives, in this unit we have also seen situations where one has to decide whether or not to take a risk in order to save people. In these cases, the *mitzvah* of *Pikuah Nefesh* is in conflict with the obligation to protect ourselves.

The Rabbis made a distinction between two types of danger: *Safek Sakanah* and *Vadai Sakanah*.

סָפֵק סַכָּנָה   *Safek Sakanah* is possible danger. If you try to save someone else, it is possible you may get hurt. Under those conditions, a person should try to save the other person.

וַדַּאי סַכָּנָה   Vadai Sakanah is certain danger, where one is likely to be killed. We are forbidden to attempt to save the other person's life if there is a good chance we will be killed. One cannot "kill oneself" to save another.

UNIT III:

שְׁמִירַת שַׁבָּת

Observing the Sabbath

In a home that follows traditional Jewish practice, these things are never done on Shabbat: driving a car, switching an electric light on or off, watching a television, playing a stereo—and many, many other things. For Jews who believe that the Torah (as interpreted by the Talmud and other books of Jewish law) forms a code of law which Jews must follow without question, each of these actions would be working on Shabbat—so they aren't done.

If you are studying from this book, chances are you are a student at a non-Orthodox Jewish school in North America, and those probably aren't the ways Shabbat is celebrated in your home. However, to understand the next unit, you'll need to understand how those rules work.

In the Torah, in the Ten Commandments, we find this rule:

> FOR SIX DAYS YOU MAY LABOR AND DO ALL YOUR WORK
> BUT THE SEVENTH DAY SHOULD BE A SABBATH
> FOR ETERNAL, YOUR GOD.
> YOU SHALL NOT DO ANY KIND OF WORK. (Exodus 20:9-10)

While this text tells us that we cannot work on Shabbat, it doesn't tell us what is work and what is not work. When we look through the rest of the Torah, we find only one specific example of a forbidden kind of work.[3]

> YOU SHALL LIGHT NO FIRE IN YOUR HOUSES ON SHABBAT. (Exodus 35:3)

Because the Rabbis had very legal minds and wanted to know exactly what was to be considered work, they carefully studied the problem and formulated a specific list. It is found in the Mishnah.

---

[3] 4. We do find another rule through a story that it is also forbidden to gather manna on Shabbat.

The following 39 categories of work are forbidden on Shabbat:

These Steps in Turning Grain into Bread: Sowing, Ploughing, Reaping, Binding Sheaves, Threshing, Winnowing, Sorting, Grinding, Sifting, Kneading, Baking.

These Steps in Turning Wool into Cloth: Shearing, Bleaching, Beating, Dyeing, Spinning, Stretching it on the Loom, Making Two Loops, Weaving Two Threads, Separating Two Threads, Tying a Knot, Untying a Knot, Sewing Two Stitches, Tearing in Order to Sew.

These Steps in Making Leather: Trapping, Slaughtering, Flaying, Salting, Curing, Scraping, Cutting.

These Steps in Writing: Writing Two Letters, Erasing in Order to Write Two Letters.

And These Steps in Construction: Building, Pulling Down, Putting Out a Fire, Lighting a Fire, Hammering, Carrying from Inside to Outside or Outside to Inside.
(Shabbat 7:2)

In the Talmud, the rabbis got even more specific about these categories, explaining that each of these is really a general category which has lots of other specific subheadings. Hundreds of actions became forbidden as work.

By traditional standards each of the following actions is forbidden on Shabbat. Here are two examples with explanations. After reviewing the examples, state which category defines the remaining actions as "work" and then explain your answers.

Ploughing	1. **Playing Soccer**
	It was feared that in kicking the ball one's foot might also cut a hole in the soil—an action which would be "ploughing" the ground, even though it wasn't intended for agricultural purposes.

Dyeing	2. **Putting a Tea Bag in Hot Water**
	Tea stains things brown. When you are putting tea in water (adding dry powder to a liquid) you are making a dye. Traditional Jews either keep tea hot all Shabbat or make a tea concentrate which they add to hot water. Once it is liquid, it is not making dye.

_____   3. Watching a Television

_____

_____

_____

_____   4. Doing Needlepoint

_____

_____

_____

_____   5. Cooking

_____

_____

_____

_____   6. Riding a Bicycle

_____

_____

_____

_____   7. Driving a Car

_____

_____

_____

_____   8. Tearing Toilet Paper

_____

_____

_____

_____ 9. Going Swimming

_____

_____

_____

_____ 10. Sharpening a Pencil

_____

_____

_____

For someone who doesn't follow these rules, Shabbat may sound a lot like being in prison (there are so many rules to follow and things you can't do). But, for Jews who give their lives over to the celebration of Shabbat, these rules make Shabbat a day of total freedom and peace. (You'd have to try it to fully understand.)

The basic idea, however, is simple. God created and made things for six days and then rested on the Seventh Day. Shabbat is when we are like God. Six days we make things, manipulate, and try to change the world. We use nature for our own purposes. On Shabbat, we leave the world alone, and change nothing—rather we let creation change us. Simply put, these 39 kinds of work are all involved in using and changing nature—resting is leaving creation alone and just experiencing it.

PROBLEM 10: THE NATURAL DISASTER

We know that Pikuah Nefesh is an important mitzvah, but what should you do when saving a human life requires you to violate another important mitzvah like observing Shabbat or Yom Kippur?

It is early Saturday morning. Your city has been hit by a severe hurricane which has caused damage to many homes and businesses. You and your family are spared, but many of your friends and their families are missing. At sunup, you go and see that your friend's house has collapsed. You had talked on the phone yesterday, and there is a good chance they are still inside. You want to go in and search for your friend and her family. You start to run back to the house to get some tools. Then you remember that is Shabbat and Jewish law forbids work on Shabbat.

Mah la'asot? What should you do? _____

_____

What is your responsibility in this matter? _____

_____

Why is this your top priority? _____

THE NATURAL DISASTER—THE JEWISH ANSWER

Problem: Your friend's life is at risk, but looking for her would be a violation of Shabbat, Which *mitzvah* should you follow, *Pikuah Nefesh* or not working on Shabbat?

Answer: Human life is more important than any other commandment. *Pikuah Nefesh* always comes first.

Reason: In Unit One, we saw this biblical verse:

> YOU SHALL KEEP MY LAWS AND MY RULES
> YOU SHALL ACT ON THEM,
> PEOPLE SHALL LIVE BY THEM. (Leviticus 18:5)

The key words in this verse are **"**PEOPLE SHALL LIVE BY THEM.**"** Even though Jews are supposed to do all the *mitzvot* (because they are commandments), one should not perform a *mitzvah* if it would mean dying. The rabbis interpret this to mean that you may break just about any commandment in order to save a human life.

In the Mishnah, the rabbis discuss a case just like ours:

> They tell us that if someone is trapped in a building that has collapsed, you are allowed to violate the Sabbath to dig for them. If at first you find only dead bodies, you must continue to dig as long as there is a little bit of hope that one person is alive. (Yoma 8:6)

Once again, *Pikuah Nefesh*, saving of a human life, is put ahead of everything else in Jewish law. You must do everything possible to find your friend and her family, providing you do not put your own life at risk.

> All purely ritual laws are suspended if there is a possibility of saving a human life—no matter how slight that possibility may be. (*Shulhan Arukh, Orekh Hayim* 329.3)

A STORY

When he was young, Hillel was poor. He had to work hard all day and earned one *tropik* a day. Every day when he went to the House of Learning he had to pay one-half *tropik* for admission. The other half *tropik* was spent on food and shelter for his family.

One Friday, Hillel could find no work. Because he had no money, the guard at the House of Learning would not let him in. Serious about learning, he climbed up on the school roof and listened through a skylight. It was December, and snow started falling.

The next morning when Rabbi Shemayah and Rabbi Avtalion came into the school, they saw the shadow of a man frozen against the skylight. They rushed up and found Hillel. The only way to save his life was to light a fire, but it was now Shabbat. They brought him down, lit a fire, and placed him before it. They said, "We should violate the Shabbat for this man." (Yoma 35b)

You should violate one Shabbat to save a person's life so that person can observe many Shabbatot. (Yoma 85b)

What is the main message of this story?

_____

_____

Health Care

These cases all involve times when the best way of healing a sick or injured person and the laws of Jewish practice seem to conflict. *Mah la-asot?* What should be done?

1. A person is very sick, and it is likely that he will die unless he is given a medicine which has been made from the blood of non-kosher animals. Normally, a Jew is not permitted to consume this.

2. A person is sick. While there is no danger that she will die from this illness, the best cure involves a medicine which has been made from the blood of non-kosher animals. Normally, a Jew is not permitted to consume this.

3. Using an X-ray machine will be a violation of Shabbat because it involves using electricity (and is in a sense kindling a fire). If two kids were fooling around on Saturday afternoon in their bedroom and one of them fell and perhaps broke her wrist, can it be x-rayed and set on Shabbat?

4. A person is hurt in a very bad fall on Saturday afternoon. There may be internal bleeding. There may be a need to operate immediately if a broken rib has punctured a lung. To determine the seriousness of the damage X rays are needed. May X rays be taken on Shabbat?

5. This is another famous case. The year was 1848. The place was Vilna, Poland. The date was just a couple of days before Yom Kippur. The problem was a plague (a cholera epidemic). It was believed by medical authorities that fasting on Yom Kippur might weaken people and lead to more people getting sick. It was believed by some religious leaders that fasting on Yom Kippur with the community really praying together could help a lot of people get and stay well. Israel Salanter was the chief rabbi. He had to make a decision whether to (a) tell people to fast, (b) tell people to eat, or (c) not take a public stand. Which was the right course?

PROBLEM 11: THE MUDDY HORSE

We've already learned that Pikuah Nefesh is an important enough mitzvah to allow you to violate Shabbat and other ritual commandments, but what about Tza'ar Ba'alei Hayyim? Can you violate Shabbat to prevent an animal from suffering or losing its life?

One Shabbat afternoon, you are taking a walk and a find a horse which has fallen into quicksand. The horse will die unless you help it. The only way you can think to save the horse is to break a board off a fence and use it as a tool. This would violate Shabbat.

Mah la'asot? What should you do? _____

_____

Do you have a responsibility in this matter? Explain. _____

_____

THE MUDDY HORSE—THE JEWISH ANSWER

Problem: It is Shabbat. You see a horse in danger of losing its life. In order to save it, you must violate Shabbat by breaking a board from a nearby fence. This is a kind of work that is strictly forbidden on Shabbat.

Answer: Save the horse.[4]

Reason: Keeping the horse from suffering and dying is a good enough reason to break Shabbat. In the *Kitzur Shulḥan Arukh,* we find these two rules:

> A fresh wound that causes suffering to the animal may be smeared with oil on Shabbat. But if the wound is healing already, and the smearing is only for the animal's comfort, it may not be done. (Kitzur Shulḥan Arukh, Book 3, 87:23)

> If one's animal suffers from overfeeding on Shabbat, one may cause it to trot in the courtyard, so that the exercise may relieve it. If it suffers from bleeding, one may let it stand in cold water. If it is bleeding and it is feared that it will die without treatment, then one may treat it. (Kitzur Shulḥan Arukh, Book 3, 87:23)

> In this same chapter, we also learn that is a *mitzvah* to have cows milked on Shabbat (even though this is work) because not milking them would be cruel, cause them pain, and put their lives at risk. (Kitzur Shulḥan Arukh, Book 3, 87.23)

---

[4]Actually, we have given the more liberal of the traditional answers to the question which Jewish law leaves unresolved. The question is complicated, stemming from a Talmudic debate about whether or not *Tza'ar Ba'alei Ḥayyim* is a "biblical" or "rabbinic" injunction. Those who believe the *mitzvah* is biblical would violate Shabbat to prevent pain, those who believe it is rabbinical would say that a human *mitzvah* cannot take precedence over a biblical injunction. This is complicated. If you want to see a full discussion, see J. David Bleich, *Contemporary Halakhic Problems, Vol. III,* KTAV (1989).

PROBLEM 12: THE ACCIDENT

We've already learned that a person can violate Shabbat to save a human life, but can Shabbat be violated to prevent possible injury?

You are in a Jewish summer camp where Shabbat is observed in a traditional way—no one drives in or out of camp, you do not turn on lights, the phone does not ring—it is truly a day of leisure and rest. On Friday night, someone is in an accident and needs to be taken to the hospital. The person is in great pain and is bleeding, but his life is not immediately at risk. With good first aid, he can probably wait until after Shabbat. The only way to get to the hospital is to drive.

Mah la'asot? **What should you do?** _____

_____

What is your responsibility in this matter? _____

_____

THE ACCIDENT—THE JEWISH ANSWER

Problem: It is Shabbat. Someone in camp has been injured and must be driven to the hospital. This is a clear violation of Shabbat.

Answer: Take the person to the hospital.

Reason: One of the forbidden categories of work on Shabbat is lighting a fire. Operating a car or motor vehicle is forbidden because each explosion of the gas in the cylinder is similar to lighting a fire. However, in the case of saving a human life or lighting a fire, it is more important to save a human life, so go ahead and drive the person to the hospital. The same is true of contributing to human healing or eliminating human pain. A modern Orthodox scholar, J. David Bleich, explains this way:

> Shabbat regulations are suspended not only for the actual treatment of an injury or illness, but also to alleviate fear, aggravation, or anxiety of a seriously ill person...(for example) even if other doctors are present, a physician may drive on Shabbat in order to visit a seriously ill patient if the patient has confidence in him and requests his presence. (J. David Bleich, *Contemporary Halakhic Problems*, Ktav (1977) p. 136)

Once again, we are applying the principle of *Pikuah Nefesh*, saving a soul.

ADDITIONAL COMPLICATIONS

Once you are at the hospital and the injured person is getting proper care, can you drive back to camp?

_____

_____

Suppose that the car that took the injured person to the hospital was the only working vehicle in camp and you were the only licensed driver. Would the situation change?

_____

_____

PROBLEM 13: THE POWER LINE

So far we've learned that one can violate Shabbat in order to save a human life, or in order to see to it that a sick person gets better, but are we permitted to violate Shabbat in order prevent possible harm?

Friday night in Jerusalem, there is a big wind storm. A power line blows down. There is electrical current in the wire, and there is a great danger that if someone touches it he or she will die. It is now early Saturday morning; soon local residents will be coming out of their homes to go to synagogue, visit family and friends, and do all the other things they do on Shabbat.

Mah la'asot? **What should be done?** _____

_____

Why is this the right answer? _____

_____

THE POWER LINE—THE JEWISH ANSWER

Problem: A fallen power line represents grave and serious danger. Can workers violate Shabbat in order to remove the danger?

Answer: Yes (but with an explanation).

Reason: This question was debated in the mid-1970's, and two conflicting opinions were stated.

> Rabbi Joshua Neuwirth argued: "Fallen lines or exposed wires are clearly dangerous to human life. Any necessary steps to eliminate this danger may be taken." (Siddur Minhat Yerushalayim, Divrei Refu'ah be-Shabbat, Otzar ha-Poskim [1977])

> Rabbi Pinhas Epstein argued: "Shabbat need not be violated because the danger to human life can be eliminated by placing a danger sign or posting a human guard. Because people can be protected without violating Shabbat, Shabbat may not be broken." (Siddur Minhat Yerushalayim, Divrei Refu'ah be-Shabbat, Otzar ha-Poskim [1977])

Both rabbis agree that Shabbat can be violated if necessary to protect humans from possible danger. They disagree on whether or not people can be protected in this case without working on Shabbat. In reviewing this dispute Rabbi J. David Bleich writes:

> In the *Shulhan Arukh* (Orekh Hayyim 334:27), we find the case of a glowing coal which fell into the public way and was located in a place where people could be harmed. Permission is given to violate Shabbat and put the coal out. No suggestion is made that they should place a guard for protection and not violate Shabbat. (J. David Bleich, *Contemporary Halakhic Problems*, KTAV [1977] p. 135)

Which rabbi do you side with? Why?

_____

_____

Note: On January 3, 1992, a snowstorm hit Jerusalem, and power went out in much of the city. The Chief Rabbi of Israel gave the power crews permission to work over Shabbat in order to insure that every household could be adequately heated. This was an act of Pikuah Nefesh.

OBSERVING SHABBAT—SUMMARY

In the last few lessons, you have seen how important observing the Sabbath is to the Jewish people. Jewish law takes Shabbat very seriously, and for many Jews this is an important *mitzvah*. We have also seen that *Pikuah Nefesh* and *Tza'ar Ba'alei Hayyim* may provide valid reasons to violate Shabbat.

UNIT IV:
נֶפֶשׁ מִפְּנֵי נֶפֶשׁ
PROBLEM 14: THE ARMED BURGLAR

We know that it is a person's obligation to save human life, but can one take another person's life in order to save oneself?

One night you are home alone. You hear someone breaking into your house. You are scared. There is a gun in the house available to you.[5]

Mah la'asot? What should you do to defend yourself? _____

_____

What are you responsibilities at this moment? _____

_____

Suppose you have the ability to kill someone. Is this justified in a case where you are home alone and an armed attacker breaks into your home? _____

_____

[5]Guns should not be accessible when there are children in the house. If guns are in the home, they should be locked away.

THE ARMED BURGLARY—THE JEWISH ANSWER

Problem: You are home alone and a burglar enters your house. You do not know if he or she is armed. You must defend yourself.

Answer: If it is the best way to protect yourself, you may use the gun and kill the person who is breaking in. This is considered self-defense and not murder.

Reason: In the Torah, we are told that a homeowner can kill anyone breaking into his or her house and it is considered to be an act of self-defense:

> IF THE THIEF IS SEIZED WHILE BREAKING IN, AND HE IS BEATEN TO DEATH, THERE IS NO BLOOD GUILT. BUT IF THEY WAIT UNTIL MORNING AND THEN KILL HIM, THERE IS BLOOD GUILT. (Exodus 22:1)

> The Rabbis explain that a thief, whether armed or unarmed, must be feared both as a thief and as a potential killer. You are therefore allowed to engage in self-defense against the attacker. The attacker is called *ha-Rodef*, the One-Who-Pursues. (Mekhilta Mishpatim 13)

In the Talmud, the Rabbis explain:

> What is the reason that one may kill a burglar? Because the thief must be thinking, "If I go in there, the owner will try to stop me, but if he does, I'll kill him." So this is how the Torah reasons "If he has come to kill you, then you act first and kill him..."

> But if it is clear to you "as the sun" that his intentions are peaceful, do not kill him. (Sanhedrin 72a)

The rules of the Talmud were written in ancient times when there were no telephones or guns, and society was very different. What is the best thing to do today when you hear a burglar in the house?

_____

_____

Gun control advocates argue that guns which are kept at home for defense more often injure residents than burglars. Guns cause accidents. Guns are used in family fights when anger takes over. What do you think the Rabbis would say about gun control?

_____

_____

PROBLEM 15: ARE YOU A HERO

We've already learned that we may kill in order to save ourselves, but may we kill in order to save a third party?

You are walking down the street. You see a woman being chased by a big man holding a knife.

Mah la'asot? What should you do? _____

_____

Do you have responsibility in this matter? If so, what is it? If not, why not? _____

_____

ARE YOU A HERO?—THE JEWISH ANSWER

Problem: You see a woman being chased by a man with a big knife. Her life is at risk, but to save her you must (1) risk your own life, and (2) possibly harm *ha-Rodef* (the pursuer). What should you do?

Answer: You have an obligation to stop the attacker and save the person being chased. If necessary, you may kill the pursuer.

Reason: Once again this is a case of *ha-Rodef*, the one who pursues. The Talmud explains that you are required to stop a *Rodef who* is trying to kill, sexually abuse, or kidnap another person.

> The following must be prevented from committing their crime, even if they must be killed to do so: a person who pursues another to kill him or her and a person who pursues another in order to commit rape.
>
> You may not kill a person to prevent him or her from sexually abusing an animal, violating Shabbat, or worshiping idols. (Sanhedrin 8:7)

Once again, this is a question of *Pikuah Nefesh*. But another idea is clearly at work.

What would happen if the chaser turned around and started to pursue you? What should you do? ___

_____

_____

PROBLEM 16: GO AHEAD, MAKE MY DAY

A Jew is permitted to kill a person in order to protect his or her own life, or in order to save another person's life, but what happens if it isn't absolutely necessary to kill a pursuer?

A woman sees a man chasing another man with a knife. The pursuer is saying, "If I catch you, I am going to kill you." The one who is being chased is running faster than the man who is chasing him.

The woman pulls a gun out of her purse and kills the chaser. The case comes to court. Three witnesses all testify that the woman could have saved the first man easily by only shooting the chaser in the leg.

Mah la'asot? **What should be the verdict?**_____

_____

_____

Why? _____

_____

_____

Go Ahead Make My Day—The Jewish Answer

Problem: A woman kills a man who has been chasing someone and threatening to kill him. Is she guilty of murder?

Answer: Yes, the woman is guilty.

Reason: You only have the right to kill *ha-Rodef if* that is the only sure way of stopping him. If taking his life was not necessary in order to save the victim, then *Pikuah Nefesh* takes over.

> If a person was pursuing another in order to kill him or her, and the person being chased could have clearly saved him or herself by maiming or injuring the pursuer, but instead chose to kill the pursuer, the one who killed the pursuer is guilty of murder and subject to the death penalty. (Sanhedrin 74a)

In this case, the woman was acting against society. The Talmudic law specifically states that one may kill *ha-Rodef* if the person is actively trying to kill you, sexually abuse you, or kidnap you. However, if there is any way you can preserve the life of *ha-Rodef,* you must do so. You cannot simply kill him when there is an alternative. This is a crime.

PROBLEM 17: ONE CANTEEN OF WATER

This is a famous case from the Talmud, and it brings back an old question—what happens if you have to risk your life to save someone else?

You and your friend are on a hike in the desert. You suddenly discover that your canteen is full and your friend's canteen, which has been leaking, is empty. It is several days' walk until the next water hole. You do not have enough water for both of you to make it. It is absolutely clear that if you try to share your water, both of you will die.

Mah la'asot? **What should you do?** _____

_____

_____

What is your primary responsibility in this matter? _____

_____

_____

one canteen of water—the Jewish answer

Problem: You and your friend are in the desert. You only have one canteen of water between you, If you both drink, you will both die; if you do not share your water, you will surely live.

Answer: Keep your own water.

Reason: If you were to share your water, or give it to your friend, you would put yourself in certain danger, *Vadai Sakanah*. This is not allowed.

This is based on a verse in the Torah, "THAT YOUR BROTHER MAY LIVE WITH YOU" (Leviticus 25:36).

Two Talmudic Rabbis argued, "It is better that they both drink it and die together rather than one person having to witness his friend's death."

Rabbi Akiba disagreed. He said, "You are not to share the water because of what it teaches in Leviticus 25:36: 'That your brother may live with you.' This means that your life comes before the life of another person."

Rabbi Akiba won the debate.

Does the situation change if you are a person who is single and has no family obligations and your friend has a family? _____

_____

_____

PROBLEM 18: KILL OR BE KILLED

We just learned that if you have to make a choice, your own life comes first. But is this always the case? May you take an innocent life in order to save your own?

Someone threatens your life. They put one gun in your hand and a second gun at your head. You are told that you must kill someone else or you will be killed.

Mah la'asot? **What should you do?** _____

_____

_____

What are your responsibilities in this matter? _____

_____

_____

KiLL OR BE KiLLED—THE JEWiSH ANSWER

Problem: Someone threatens to kill you if you do not kill another person.

Answer: You must let yourself be killed.

Reason: You may do almost anything to save your life; however, you cannot be guilty of murder, rape, or idolatry.

This again is an example of אֵין דּוֹחִין נֶפֶשׁ מִפְּנֵי נֶפֶשׁ *ein dohin nefesh mip'nei nefesh,* we don't take one life in order to save another.

The only time it is permissible to kill another person is in defense of a human life, or to prevent sexual abuse or kidnapping. You cannot be a judge between yourself and another person. There is no way of deciding which is more valuable. The Talmud explains it this way:

> A certain man came to Rava and said to him, "The governor of my town has ordered me to kill someone and has warned me that if I do not do so he will have me killed. What am I to do?"

> Rava replied, "Let yourself be killed but do not kill him. How do you know that your blood is redder? Perhaps the blood of that man is redder." (Pesahim, 25b)

Test cases

This is a true story of the Holocaust. The night before Rosh ha-Shanah at Auschwitz the Nazis gathered 1400 teenage boys and placed them in a holding cell. They were to be killed in the gas chambers 24 hours later. A group of Kapos (Jewish guards) watched the boys. Soon the bribes began. Jewish parents took the gold and diamonds they had hidden away and used them to bribe the Kapos to release their sons. Because the Kapos were responsible for delivering precisely 1400 prisoners the next day, they took a new boy as hostage before they released each redeemed son.

An inmate came to one of the rabbis and asked his permission to redeem his son. What answer should the rabbi give?

Mah la'asot? _____

_____

_____

In the movie Terminator 2, there is a similar problem. A scientist who is a good person is about to make a scientific discovery which will eventually cause many people to be killed. If the scientist is killed before he makes his discovery, many lives will be saved. Sarah wants to kill the scientist, but her son stops her. Even though many human lives will be saved, he feels that killing people except in self-defense is wrong. Earlier the son tells the robot, the T-2000, "You just can't go around killing people!" The robot asks why, and the boy answers, "You've just gotta take my word on this."

Who is right? Can you kill one innocent person in order to save thousands or even millions?

Mah la'asot? _____

_____

_____

57

Two Talmudic Stories

These two stories from the Talmud raise different questions:

What should one do if a group of Jews was walking along a road and was stopped by a group of pagans who said to them: "Give us one of you to kill or we will kill all of you."

The right thing to do is to refuse to surrender anyone, and let all of them die together, rather than surrendering one Jewish soul. But if the pagans single out one person by name, as they once did in the case of Sheva ben Bikhri, that person should be surrendered to them, so that the others may be saved. Rabbi Simeon ben Lakish explained: "Only someone who is under sentence of death, the way Sheva ben Bikhri was, can be turned over." But Rabbi Yohanan disagreed: "Anyone singled out by name may be turned over." (Jerusalem Talmud, Terumot 8:12)

Ulla bar Koshev was being sought by the Roman government. He was hiding in Lod at the home of Rabbi Joshua ben Levi. The government laid siege to the town and said that the city would be destroyed if they didn't turn him over. Rabbi Joshua convinced Ulla to give himself up (in order to save the city). Up to that point, the prophet Elijah would visit Rabbi Joshua every day. After that day, he never came again. The rabbi fasted for several days. Finally, Elijah reappeared and said to the Rabbi: "I don't reveal myself to informers!" Rabbi Joshua said, "But I just followed the Mishnah's teachings." Elijah then said, "Is this a teaching for righteous Jews?" (Jerusalem Talmud, Terumot 8:12)

These two stories from the same page in the Jerusalem Talmud have very different feelings about *ein dohin nefesh mip'nei nefesh*, we don't reject one life in order to save another. What are the differences? Where do they agree? Why can Jewish law represent two opinions which contradict each other?

_____

_____

PROBLEM 19: A PREGNANT MOTHER

We've learned that if one person is chasing a second to kill him or her we are allowed—in fact, required—to kill the pursuer in order to save the life of the person being chased. That pursuer was doing something wrong on purpose. What happens when an unborn child threatens a mother's life?

A pregnant mother has a medical complication. The doctor must make a choice. She can only save one life. Which life should be saved—the mother's or the unborn child's?

Mah la'asot? **What should be done?** _____

_____

What is your reasoning? _____

_____

A PREGNANT MOTHER—THE JEWISH ANSWER

Problem: A pregnant mother has a medical complication and the doctor must make a choice about whom to save, the baby or the mother.

Answer: If the mother's life is in danger, one must abort the fetus if that will take her out of harm's way.

Reason: In Jewish law, this unborn child is compared to *ha-Rodef,* the one who pursues. It is as if the unborn child is chasing after the mother's life. If it is a choice between the two, then it is the mother who is to be saved.

The Jewish tradition teaches us a couple of important things about abortion. The first is that abortion is not murder. In the Torah we are told:

> IF TWO MEN FIGHT AND ONE OF THEM PUSHES A PREGNANT WOMAN AND A MISCARRIAGE RESULTS, THE RESPONSIBLE PARTY SHOULD PAY DAMAGES TO THE WOMAN'S HUSBAND. BUT IF THE WOMAN DIES FROM THE PUSH, IT SHALL BE CONSIDERED MANSLAUGHTER (POTENTIALLY A CAPITAL CRIME). (Exodus 21:22-23)

This passage shows us that the Torah considers the accidental loss of life as a kind of "murder," while an accidental abortion was considered a personal injury, not murder. For the Jewish tradition, abortion is not murder. It is the taking of a potential life, not the taking of a life.

When the Talmud discusses this very choice between saving a mother's life or saving a fetus's potential life, it says:

> If a woman is having difficulty giving birth, the fetus within her womb may be aborted because her life takes precedence over its potential life. But if the greater part of the baby has already been born, it may not be touched, for we do not take one life to save another's. (Oholot 7:6)

> A fetus in the process of being born which puts its mother's life at risk is considered to be *ha-Rodef* and must be aborted until the moment when its head emerges. After this, it cannot be killed, because it is not permitted to take one human life to save another. But isn't the emerging baby still a pursuer? No, at that point heaven is the pursuer. (Sanhedrin 72b)

In the Jerusalem Talmud, they explain why abortion is not allowed once the head emerges this way:

> At this point we do not know if the fetus is pursuing the mother or the mother pursuing the fetus. (Talmud Jerushalayim, Sanhedrin 8.9, 26c)

In the end, the basic principle here is: *ein dohin nefesh mip'nei nefesh*, we don't take one life in order to save another. For the Jewish tradition, abortion is not murder, and it must clearly be done if the mother's life is at risk.

PROBLEM 20: ABORTION COMPLICATIONS

So far we've learned that Jewish law does not consider abortion to be murder and that it does endorse abortion when the mother's life is at risk, but what about abortion under other circumstances?

The following women are seeking abortions. All of them are less than three months pregnant.

a. Janet is a 16-year-old who has become pregnant by mistake. She is not in love with her boyfriend and has no intention of keeping the baby if it is born. Going through with the pregnancy will cause her great distress and perhaps ruin her educational future.

b. Barbara is a 43-year-old mother of two. Both she and her husband have good jobs, and her youngest child is seven years old. This pregnancy was an accident. Barbara and her husband could afford another child, and theirs is loving family that is stable. However, neither of them wants to deal with another infant—they feel too old.

c. Deborah was raped. She is carrying the fetus of her rapist. It is causing her much distress, and she doubts that she could ever love this child. She also worries about the harm all her hate and anger is doing to the fetus. She wants an abortion in order to put all this behind her.

d. Susan is 41 years old. She and her husband very much want a child. Because of her age her doctor recommended amniocentesis. The tests showed that the baby will be genetically defective and will be born with profound retardation. The doctor has recommended an abortion.

e. Chanel is 32 years old. She is unmarried and is not involved in a long-term relationship. She is not even certain who is the father. She has had two previous abortions. When asked why she wanted this abortion, Chanel answered, "Would it be fair to any kid to have me as its mother?" It is suspected that Chanel has a substance abuse problem.

Mah la'asot? **In which cases (if any) should an abortion be permitted?**

_____

_____

_____

ABORTION COMPLICATIONS—THE JEWISH ANSWER

Problem: Is abortion permitted when the life of the mother is not at stake, but there are other serious concerns?

Answer: It depends on who you ask.

Reason: The abortion question is caught between two opposing Jewish values—different rabbis have interpreted it different ways.

One position believes that even though abortion is not considered a murder, it is not considered a good thing. In the *Zohar*, a mystical Jewish book, that idea is very clearly stated:

> Abortion is one of three things which increases the distance between God and people and causes prayers to be unanswered. The Holy-One-Who-is-to-Be-Blessed weeps for the loss. (Zohar, Shemot)

Even though abortion does not carry a penalty, one Jewish school of thought teaches that it is always wrong. Sometimes it may be necessary to save another life, but it is always wrong. Some rabbis argue that it violates one of the seven laws which God taught Noah for all humanity (not just Jews):

> WHOEVER SHEDS THE BLOOD OF A HUMAN, BY A HUMAN SHALL HIS BLOOD BE SHED. GOD MADE PEOPLE IN GOD'S IMAGE. (Genesis 9:6)

The idea here is that even though an abortion is not murder, it is spilling human blood and destroying God's image. Based on this view, many authorities accept no abortions except in cases where the mother's life is at risk.

A second school of thought teaches that abortion is not desirable, but is acceptable in a number of situations. Some of these teachings:

> As long as the fetus has not emerged from the womb, even if not to save the mother's life, but only to save her from the great pain and harassment that the fetus causes, an abortion is permissible. (Rabbi Jacob Emden, Responsa Maharit, 1:99)

> If a mother has serious needs, even if they are not vital, an abortion is permissible.
> (Rabbi Benzion Meir Hai Uziel, Mishpotai Uziel)

There are two principles involved here, *Tza'ara D'gufah Kadim,* avoiding her pain; and *Pikuah Nefesh,* saving a life. In trying to find the "right thing" to do in each case, the rabbis try to balance these two concerns. Different rabbis have found the "balancing point" in different places; that is why there are differing "authentic" answers.

Extreme cases

The Holocaust generated a lot of ethical questions. Here are two more:

1. During the occupation of Poland, a German officer impregnated a Jewish woman. He took her to a Jewish doctor and demanded that he perform an abortion. The doctor refused. The German officer then took out his pistol and told the doctor, "Either perform the abortion or I will kill you." What should the doctor do? (Rabbi Isser Yehudah Unterman, No'am VI, 52)

2. In 1942, in the Kovno Ghetto, the Nazis issued a decree that every pregnant Jewish woman would be killed along with her fetus. Women went to doctors and asked them to abort their fetuses so that they could live. What should the doctor do? (Ephraim Oshry, Mi-Ma'amakim)

ISSUES OF SELF-DEFENSE—SUMMARY

הָרוֹדֵף   In Judaism, the use of violence in self-defense is always permissible. The principle is called *ha-Rodef*, The One Who-Pursues. It states that a person can stop a *Rodef* who is trying to kill, kidnap, or sexually assault in order to protect the victim, whether it is someone else or yourself.

Halakhah has a second insight about stopping *ha-Rodef*. It says in the Mishnah, "The following must be prevented from committing their crime...." In a sense, you are doing the pursuer a favor by preventing his or her crime and not adding to his or her sins.

We also learn, however, that if *ha-Rodef* can be stopped without being killed, that his or her death is wrong, an excessive use of force.

אֵין דוֹחִין נֶפֶשׁ מִפְּנֵי נֶפֶשׁ   The principle of *ein dohin nefesh mip'nei nefesh* states that we don't reject one life in order to save another. This is the rabbis' rejection of "the lifeboat scenario" and states that no person can choose whose life is more valuable. In those cases, we do not choose. We also learn that if there is a choice, you must always affirm the sanctity of your own life first—and choose it.

The principle of *ein dohin nefesh mip'nei nefesh* also teaches that one may not take an innocent life in order to save one's own.

צַעֲרָא דְגוּפָא קָדִים פְּקוּחַ נֶפֶשׁ   Finally, in our discussion of abortion we learned that *halakhah* does not always provide exact answers and that here the rabbis struggle to balance two values: *Tza'ara D'gufah Kadim*, avoiding her pain; and our old friend, *Pikuah Nefesh*, saving a soul.

MAH LA'ASOT

For the last few weeks you have had the experience of going through a book which has forced you to make choices. You learned that many of the choices we make as Jewish people are rooted in Jewish tradition, notably the Torah, and explained in the Talmud. You have even had an opportunity to try to reason like some of the rabbis in the Talmud.

We recognize that not all of the choices you had to make were easy. There really were no right or wrong answers, just choices between two important things.

There is an old Yiddish saying, *"Shyer tzu sein a Yid.* It's hard to be a Jew." We suspect you now understand more of what this means. We hope when you are confronted with choices in your life, the Jewish tradition will make a difference. Good luck!